MONEY MANAGEMENT FOR STUDENTS

Doris T. Berry

Copyright © 2022 Doris T. Berry

COPYWRIGHT TEMPLATE
All rights reserved. No part of this publication may be reproduced, distributed, or transmitted in any form or by any means, including photocopying, recording, or other electronic or mechanical methods, without the prior written permission of the publisher, except in the case of brief quotations embodied in critical reviews and certain other noncommercial uses permitted by copyright law.

CONTENTS

Title Page
Copyright
Foreword
Chapter 1: 1
Chapter 2: 4
Chapter 3: 8
Chapter 4: 11
Chapter 5: 13
Chapter 6: 16
Chapter 7: 18
Chapter 8: 21
Chapter 9: 23
Chapter 10: 25

FOREWORD

One of the secrets to reducing debts while studying is to conserve money and spend less. Whether you are studying abroad or not, it is crucial to keep saving money as this might provide you peace of mind after you have graduated and started paying your obligations related to your education. This may also assist you in avoiding certain financial troubles. This book will discuss the usual tactics for saving and spending while studying.

CHAPTER 1:

What Makes Financial Management Important for Students?

◆ ◆ ◆

Synopsis

While most students depart with significant debts and some with trim, the amount of debt incurred will rely on how effectively you have managed your costs while still studying. If you don't want to pay for a significant deficit and save money while you are a student, you need to know how to handle finance is crucial. Through financial management, you will not only be able to save money from paying the enormous debt but also limit your spending and prevent running out of budget while you are still studying.

The Significance Of Money Management For Students.

Managing your finances is crucial, particularly for people who don't have enough money to pay for their courses. Although students regard this duty as hard to perform, it is good to master the fundamentals of money management as this may also provide you with a better future. For you to be effective in financial planning, here are some of the things you should take note of:

• You should permanently save a percentage of what you have earned from your part-time work or student loan cheques. You may try investing part of it to follow your passion for generating more money.

• As a student, you should also stay informed about the current economic cycle since this refers to the optimum periods to borrow money. There are instances where the interest is low. Find out when the interest rates are high if you want to discover the optimum time to invest or reinvest your money.

• You should grasp the payout of picking one chance over another. You should also know your financial net worth, especially when making financial choices like accepting part-time employment and needless purchases.

• You also learn how to build your financial objectives, weather setbacks, and make realistic strategies.

• Taking advantage of the assets that are tax-sheltered while you are still young via the programs of job perks is also a wonderful thing.

• Developing crucial financial competence in earning, saving, spending, and recognizing the economic situation may also reward you.

Perks Of Managing Finance.

Regarding personal financial concerns, many college students rely on certain family members or parents to aid, while others squander student loans immediately. One of the rewards you may experience from managing finance is that you can save and manage money effectively. With this, you will be able to have additional capital, which you may utilize for vital things like projects.

There are more things you might experience after you have learned how to handle your funds. If you want to be successful in the future, this might be your stepping stone. Although money management is not a simple thing to undertake, this may be done every day. Financial management is a step-by-step procedure. This can't be done quickly, particularly if you don't mind spending money since you know you can pay your debts after getting a job. If you find it hard to manage your finances, asking for some ideas from your friends or anybody you know might also be helpful.

CHAPTER 2:

The Best Ways to Budget Your Money

◆ ◆ ◆

Synopsis

Entering college may seem thrilling for some individuals. But, others find it a scary undertaking for many reasons. Graduating high school and joining a university or college is a significant step. Many kids frequently taste independence from the real world and go forth from the protection and security of their families.

Various things need to be juggled so that the college of students will be successful. From attending courses and studying to managing and networking funds, there's plenty that college students should consider. One of them is to spend money carefully.

Money Management Techniques.

Spending intelligently is not something that most students do. Often, folks spend money without thinking about their budget or the ramifications of spending a significant amount of cash. If you want to be wise with spending money while you are studying, here are some of the techniques you may take into consideration:

· Enroll in Meal Plans.

One of the ways to save money is by subscribing to meal plans. A meal plan is a program that is pre-paid. This is where you pay a set amount of money for your meals on your campus every semester. In addition to that, meal plans are convenient. You may select your snack or lunch anytime you want, and you don't need to prepare it yourself.

· Share Expenses with a Roommate.

Another option you might explore while cutting your studying expenditures is splitting expenses with a roommate. If you live in a dorm, you should assume that you will live in a tight quarter with other students. Many expenditures might be divided between your roommate. Some of them are food and furniture.

· Watch out for impulsive purchases.

Spending money on items you enjoy but don't need might be tempting. It is crucial to change your expenditures since you will require cash for other critical things like apparel and education.

Supplies and books. Instead of spending your cash on these products, check your expenditures. Then, utilize this on those you truly need the most for your everyday existence.

· Recognize what is necessary and not necessary.

Another thing that most students can't accomplish is to distinguish the difference between their necessities from their desires. Because of having little information about non-essential and vital, some students squander their money on certain products that will merely waste their money.

Essential things such as hygiene goods, clothes, and food are needed for everyday existence. Non-essential items, on the other hand, may include electrical devices, a movie trip, or a pair of shoes when you already have multiple teams. Even though this might be challenging at first, restricting your spending is crucial as this will enable you off certain items that you don't need for your budget.

• **Lowering the cost of certain supplies.**

Saving money from supplies might be simple, especially if you live on campus. Before you walk directly to the university bookstore, you could browse around neighboring bookshops for you to know whether they are significantly cheaper or not. With this, you may save money on the textbooks you will utilize for the following semester. In addition, you may save yourself even more money if you select downloading your book to a tablet device or an e-book. If you are trying to hold on to certain products like 3-ring binders as well as loose leaf paper, consider getting in bulk from a business that provides

Office supplies. Retailers grant you a discount when you buy a Huge quantity of goods. If everything fails, try internet sites. This might assist you in saving money by examining deals.

In conclusion.

CHAPTER 2:

Knowing how to spend intelligently may be challenging. But, this might provide you with rewards in the long term. If this is your first time managing your finances, those described techniques above might aid you colossal time. If you can't control your costs efficiently, stay away from areas that stimulate you to acquire products that are not required for your everyday existence. Take notice that there's a distinction between understanding what you desire and need. So, be clever with your money while studying since this allows you to save an abundant amount of money, which you can use for your future costs or other vital objectives.

CHAPTER 3:

Innovative Cost-Cutting Strategies

◆ ◆ ◆

Synopsis

Cutting down spending is not straightforward for some. However, this is vital, especially for people who don't want to wind up having any money for the upcoming weeks. The process of reducing expenditures can be done by contemplating inventive solutions, which are excellent for everyone, no matter what institution or university they are into and how much money they have.

There are various options you may explore for reducing your expenditures while learning. With them, you can assure that you will be able to experience discounts. Below are some of the unique ideas you may take into consideration:

Planning your budget might assist you in cutting down your spending. This not only enables you to put down your weekly or daily spending, but you will also be able to check whether there are any items you can cut.

Innovative Ways To Reduce Your Expenses While Studying.

If you don't know how to plan your budget, there's a terrific approach for you to create one. First and foremost, you should know your budget. Then, list your everyday costs. Limiting oneself to a specific expenditure every day is a brilliant idea. This will also restrict you from purchasing products that you will not every day. Once you have prepared your budget, you may save much money.

Just make the necessary purchases.

Purchasing just what you need is also a brilliant idea to reduce spending. When buying, decide whether it is a necessity or a desire. Once you have concluded that it is a desire, dismiss it. Buy just what you need since this may minimize your expense.

Making Smart Book Purchases.

Textbooks are highly significant for your study. However, cutting down your expenditures does not imply that you don't need to acquire books. You may purchase your essential textbooks. But, search for other outlets that will provide discounts or lower prices for your important books. With this, you will be able to decrease your spending as you will receive inexpensive textbooks of the same quality as costly ones.

Utilize special offers.

As a student, there's also an excellent opportunity to get savings. Some establishments or shops might give you discounts. Even some shops provide

10% discounts or below is still a huge issue, particularly if you want to save money. If you are not fond of local shopping, various websites might give you savings. The only thing you should do is look for them on Google. If you don't know which is reputable or not, certain websites may assist you in locating such savings.

Keep Your Transportation Costs Under Control.

Regarding transportation, you don't have to own a car or a specific vehicle for everyday transit. But, if your parents give you one, you may use it occasionally. Gas may be pricey. However, you always grab discounts if there are such ones. You can use a bike instead of driving a vehicle if you have a bike. Through this, you will not only reduce the petrol expenditure, but also you will be able to get rid of traffic. If you are living near your university, walking might be an excellent option. This might also be an ideal type of workout.

Cook Your Foods or Purchase Low-Cost Foods.

Buying goods from restaurants may occasionally enhance your expenditure, enabling you to spend more than what you have allocated. So, if feasible, make meals or get inexpensive ones. This can help you save money while you are eating nutritious meals. Culinary meals at your dorm or at any place you're staying may also enable you to improve your cooking talents.

There are various ways you might do for reducing down your expenditures. If you want to be successful with what you strive for, then take this seriously and keep with your intended budget or costs, as this may make a difference.

CHAPTER 4:

Refrain from using your credit or debit card.

❖ ❖ ❖

Synopsis

The majority of college students consider getting their first credit card to be a rite of passage. This is the initial step in creating your credit. This also enables you to improve your financial freedom. But, unbeknownst to practically many students, when it comes to their possibilities in the future, having a good credit history is highly crucial, like an excellent GPA. However, students still need to learn to keep credit or debit cards away if they don't want to pay a hefty amount after or before graduation.

There's a tremendous difference between getting a credit card and applying for each credit card offer, which is made accessible to every student. If you are a student, you undoubtedly consider student loans. Therefore, do not be seduced by each free T-shirt offer you see.

How To Refrain From Using Your Credit Or Debit Card.

It is because you will find yourself with additional bills if you would make the most of your credit card. One of the main concepts of managing money is to avoid spending more cash than you can afford. If you have certain credit cards, this becomes simple to go into a significant debt, which you will have a hard time paying off.

You may consider various strategies to avoid credit or debit cards. One of these strategies is to purchase your essential products using your cash. If you still have money in your wallet or pocket, use it instead of your credit card. This will assist you in avoiding using your credit card. But this does not imply that you should not use credit cards. You may always utilize them, but do not abuse them. Abusing credit or debit cards may be a colossal disaster, especially for individuals who constantly buy stuff using these.

Another way you may try to avoid credit cards is by avoiding areas where you will be tempted to purchase essential products for your studies. Do not use credit or debit cards constantly when paying for your education. If you can pay it with cash or a loan, consider it your alternative. Though having a credit card might help you improve your credit history in the future, if you have failed to pay your obligation, this may harm your credit history and affect your credit score.

Before applying for a credit card, knowing or comprehending it is also crucial. This can assist you in contemplating avoiding the things that you should or not do to get rid of any difficulty.

CHAPTER 5:

Set up some money for emergencies.

Synopsis

Saving money should not simply be for the future costs of your schooling. You should also store money for emergency usage. This can help you avoid borrowing some money from your friends or parents. This also enables you to get away with getting a loan that might add up to your debt in the long run. So, dedicate some savings for emergency usage since this may make a difference.

How To Set Apart Money For Emergency Use.

Allocating some money for your emergency purpose may not be a simple thing to undertake. But, there are methods you may consider. These are as follows:

- **Keep a separate account for emergencies.**

You may try splitting your funds if you find it hard to save for emergency usage. You should divide part of your money for other purposes and emergency needs. This will assist you in avoiding spending the money on those items that are not necessary.

- **Place the money in your bank account.**

If you are often tempted to spend money on numerous items, put it into your bank account. Once you have deposited money to your bank account, don't check it constantly since this will offer you temptations to spend it only to buy goods, which might be additional expenditure on your budget. Therefore, if you don't want to spend saving for emergency usage for goods that are not beneficial and necessary, then deposit them directly into your bank account.

By contemplating those listed above, saving money can be done quickly. So, if you want the money, you may utilize it for emergency needs without depending on other individuals; bear in mind those mentioned above.

The Advantages Of Setting Up Money For Emergencies.

You will experience several advantages after you have earmarked a portion of your money for emergency usage. One of the advantages is that you can avoid loans, which might build up your bills. This will also enable you to avoid borrowing money from your parents or pals. The most excellent part about having money as your emergency cash is that you may spend it anytime for vital objectives. If you have this money, all you have to do is to withdraw it or obtain it in your safe.

Although designating some savings for emergency usage is not a must for all students, this may help limit their costs or debts since they will be utilizing their savings instead of their existing budget, which can be pricey.

CHAPTER 6:

Keep Spending Records in a Journal or Spreadsheet

◆ ◆ ◆

Synopsis

One of the secrets to enjoying savings while studying is documenting your expenses using a spreadsheet or a notebook. With this, tracking your costs will never be problematic for you. Monitoring your expenditures on a spreadsheet or journal may also enable you to examine the items you have spent or bought.

Tracking your expenditure is now made more accessible. Depending on your preferences, you may use your laptop or any device. You may also keep track of your expenses in your journal.

Keeping Tabs On Your Spending.

Tracking your expenditures is not a hard thing to accomplish. In truth, it is straightforward. You only need a journal, pen, or laptop if you would utilize a spreadsheet. Once they are done, the next thing you need to do is to jot down your daily costs. You can plan if you wish. By writing down your expenditures in advance, you can track down everything. Also, you will know your restrictions since you have previously allocated your money.

Remember to note down everything you have spent when recording your expenditures on a journal or spreadsheet. No matter how much you have bought, it is good to write down what you have spent.

The rationale is that this might enable you to monitor whether you have effectively planned your money or have already bought anything that costs more than what you have allocated.

Tracking what you have spent maybe a dull chore for any student. But, if you genuinely want to save money, you should start monitoring your expenditures. Besides, this is not anything that will demand too much of your time. The ideal time to monitor your spending is after you have acquired what you need or desire.

CHAPTER 7:

Earn Additional Income Online

◆ ◆ ◆

Synopsis

With today's growth of technology, getting some extra income online is now made simpler and more achievable. You may attempt to generate some additional income online if you believe your budget is insufficient and don't want to pile on your bills. With this, you will avoid borrowing money, and you may get rid of debts.

Making Money Online: Strategies.

If you desire additional money while studying, there are methods to generate some cash over the internet. Some of them are:

Consider Paid Services.

Today, some firms may pay you for doing anything. If you can create surveys, you may earn some money from them. However, be sure that your selected firm is dependable and won't need any advance money. There are various paid services that you might examine online. All you need is to hunt for some.

Sell Products Online.

You may establish your website and provide products if you want to sell things. Launching your website does not imply paying for hosting or anything that would enable you to reach your desired audience. You may try a free blogging platform like WordPress. Or, you may build a page on your Facebook account where you can showcase your provided items.

You may also try other social networking sites.

Work as a Freelancer.

Whether interested in writing or building websites, you may now enjoy the freelancing world. You might be a freelance writer or web designer. Some various firms and websites recruit freelancing. If you want to make the most of your talents, then you should not dare to skip being freelance.

This will allow you to earn some cash while developing your talents. However, while looking for a firm or website, be sure that

They are reputable or dependable. The reason is that certain websites would only utilize your expertise for fraud. So, be cautious while picking one. If you don't have any concept on which to contemplate, seek some guidance from your buddies or other persons you know.

There are other methods to earn some income online. It all depends on how you will take advantage of these possibilities. However, while generating additional income online, never neglect your academics. It would help if you still concentrate on your education while working. With this, you may generate income while receiving the most outstanding education, which might lead to your future.

CHAPTER 8:

Choose a Part-Time Position After Classes

◆ ◆ ◆

Synopsis

Every student's favorite portion of the day may be their free time. However, you may try part-time employment after courses to save some of your expenditures. This will help you generate money and will also enable you to make the most of your leisure time. So, choose part-time work if you don't want to squander your time and make some income.

Making the most of your leisure time by exploring part-time work has never been a terrible idea. This may provide numerous advantages in the long term and make you a better student. But how may you hunt for part-time jobs?

Utilizing Your Free Time By Looking Into Part-Time Jobs

There are several possibilities you may examine when it comes to part-time work. You may search locally or online. Most college students seek a crew position at a specific restaurant or business as one of the accepted part-time jobs. Numerous restaurants and culinary establishments hire part-timers. You might compare prices in your neighborhood. This may not be very comfortable for some, but after you have gotten the fruit of your labor, you will be more driven to study and take it seriously.

There are various possibilities you may take into consideration. You may explore online since numerous websites or firms hunt for part-timers. If you may select part-time work online, your schedule is more flexible, however, because you need to focus on your education. You should perform your duties after lessons, so you prevent any hassle. But, one of the things you should take notice of is the reputation and dependability of the firm you're dealing with. You can prevent people who will not pay for your services. So, if this is your first time, consider shopping all the time to deal with a reliable firm.

You have to keep in mind that producing money might be tricky. So, if you don't want to toss or spend money on things that would merely waste it, then know how to pay significance with your money and attempt to earn some of it. With this, you will be able to realize how hard it is to make money.

CHAPTER 9:

Purchasing what you need rather than what you want

◆ ◆ ◆

Synopsis

One of the easiest methods to save money is purchasing what you need, not what you desire. By distinguishing your necessities from your desires, you will be able to acquire products in a wise method. Unfortunately, not everyone realizes the difference between their requirements and desires. That is why some wind up acquiring their desires rather than their needs. So, when you purchase, the first thing you need to do is to figure out your requirements and desires.

More often than not, students opt to purchase their desires instead of their necessities. It is because, in the first place, they don't know the difference between them. Needs are things that you need for you to remain alive. Some of them are meals and apparel. Other than these, transportation and housing are also regarded to constitute one's requirements. But, they pertain to the little necessities. The concept behind it is that anybody may live and thrive in it without a home or mode of transportation as long as they feed regularly.

How To Determine Your Needs And Wants.

For students, some of their necessities may include books, clothes, snacks, and shelter. Everything else is already deemed a wish. Wants are those items that may bring pleasure or fun, like electronics. Although you also require mobile gadgets for communication and a laptop or computer to support you with homeworks, they are not considered essential. It is because different sources might provide you with knowledge, like books. You may also communicate by attempting the usual manner of speaking with people.

There are additional items that are recognized as desires. One of them is to have an automobile. There are numerous forms of transportation you might consider. You might consider utilizing your bicycle if you want to minimize petrol prices. Or, if you want to use your vehicle, always inquire whether there are discounts for students. Although not all may offer you discounts, most gas stations may provide you the possibility to save money.

Once you have chosen what you need or want, you will be able to experience savings since this may provide you the option to minimize your expenditure from obtaining your desires. So, if you don't want to pay a significant debt, try recognizing the difference between desires and necessities first.

CHAPTER 10:

Student discounts provide financial savings

◆ ◆ ◆

Synopsis

Knowing how to benefit from student discounts is crucial if you're a student. Through this, conserving money will never be demanding as you may spend less by getting the rewards of having student discounts.

Unfortunately, not all students understood how to make the most of student discounts. That is the reason why some can't save enough money while they are still studying. You have to bear in mind that you are not a student forever. So, if you're a student, consider saving money via student discounts.

Student Discount Strategies For Saving Money.

Saving money through student discounts is straightforward and may be done in simple ways. If you wish to enjoy the advantages of being a student by employing student discounts, then bear in mind the following:

Recognize stores that provide discounts to students.

Not all establishments or shops in your local region offer student discounts. You need to know the stores that give student discounts to get value. Whenever you are shopping, always inquire if they are providing discounts for discounts. Others don't dare to voice these remarks because they are bashful. But, you have to understand that there are reasons why student IDs were developed. They are not simply for your identity, but they may also be handy whelpling advantage of the discounts certain establishments give. Always carry your ID to the edge of deals if you want to save money from these reductions.

Look for discounts for students online.

Student discounts can't simply be obtained locally. With the improvement of today's technology, anybody may receive student discounts online. Some websites may assist you in searching, such as internet retailers that give low bargains or specials for students. However, be sure that your selected websites are legitimate and will provide you with actual savings. Before you make any purchase, you might consider asking some questions beforehand. This will assist you in leading in the appropriate route.

Lower-cost travel.

If you are a student who regularly travels for research reasons or enjoyment, you may travel inexpensively. More often than not, traveling may be pricey. But, if you are a student, you can travel more affordably. Some websites might guide you to cheaper flights or trips. You have to notice that traveling with student discounts also makes a difference.

Student discounts are like free money. If you want to enjoy

your life as a student, don't forget to save money with student discounts. This will provide you with the ideal experience and enable you to avail yourself of some of the goods you need at a reduced charge. So, take advantage of student discounts and save money while continuing your education.

www.ingramcontent.com/pod-product-compliance
Lightning Source LLC
Chambersburg PA
CBHW050325220526
45465CB00005B/2136